Digital Mindchanges for CEOs

What CEOs need to know to survive the Digital (R)Evolution

Sanjay Sauldie

Director of
the European Internet Marketing Institute & Academy

Any questions? Ask us anything you like!

Digital Mindchanges for CEOs

© 2015 by Sanjay Sauldie

Das vorliegende Werk ist in allen seinen Teilen urheberrechtlich geschützt. Alle Rechte vorbehalten, insbesondere das Recht der Übersetzung, des Vortrags, der Reproduktion, der Vervielfältigung auf fotomechanischem oder anderen Wegen und der Speicherung in elektronische Medien. Ungeachtet der Sorgfalt, die auf die Erstellung von Text, Abbildungen, und Programmen verwendet wurde, können weder Verlag noch Autor, Herausgeber oder Übersetzer für mögliche Fehler und deren Folgen eine juristische Verantwortung oder irgendeine Haftung übernehmen. Die in diesem Werk wiedergegebenen Gebrauchsnamen, Handelsnamen, Warenbezeichnungen usw. können auch ohne besondere Kennzeichnung Marken sein und als solche den gesetzlichen Bestimmungen unterliegen.

ISBN: 9783738601114

Herausgegeben vom
SSX - Verlag für audiovisuelle Medien, Mannheim

Lange Rötterstr. 34 - 68167 Mannheim - Germany
Telefon: +49 (0) 621 – 97 87 933
Telefax: +49 (0) 621 – 97 87 934
E-Mail: internet@ssx.de - Internet: www.ssx.de
Umschlaggestaltung: www.ssx.de
Umschlagmotiv: © 2015 www.iroi.de & Bild: © Niclas Harwart.

iROI® ist eine eingetragene Marke von Sanjay Sauldie, auch wenn im Buch der besseren Lesbarkeit wegen auf den stetigen Markenhinweis beim Begriff iROI verzichtet wurde.

Bibliografische Information der Deutschen Nationalbibliothek:

Die Deutsche Nationalbibliothek verzeichnet diese Publikation in der Deutschen Nationalbibliografie. Detaillierte bibliografische Daten sind im lnternet über http://dnb.d-nb.de abrufbar.

© 2015 Sanjay Sauldie

Herstellung und Verlag:

BoD - Books on Demand, Norderstedt

Any questions? Ask us anything you like!

Sanjay Sauldie is the developer of the iROI-Strategy and has continued optimizing the strategy for the new changes in the markets and updates the strategy daily. Over 500 small and medium-sized businesses as well as international corporations are using the knowledge and implementing the iROI-Strategy in their companies. International and national awards show the high quality of this strategy:

Even the German TÜV has checked our quality, we are the only Internet Marketing Strategy, that ever got this seal:

Free downloads and more: www.sauldie.org/vip

Dedicated to my dear parents,

who always believe in me, support me and give me the freedom to develop my own ideas.

Thank you from the bottom of my heart!

I would also like to dedicate this book to my partner and soulmate

Rita Anna Küffner,

who inspires me in my work and my life – and keeps me smiling the whole day!

Thanks for your good mood and inspiration!

Digital Mindchanges for CEOs

Dear CEO!

The number one complaint I hear from the CEOs who've been around awhile is that they are doing well, but they'd like to get to the next digital level.....FASTER! Does that sound familiar?

In my coaching programs, I've developed a system called the IROI-Strategy. That will help you develop your business faster and sounder, and then perform Online Business Optimization up to Digital Leadership.

Let's join hands and do that together! More details you will find in these guidelines. I wish you a very successful journey through the world of Internet Marketing. You will get some important Mindchanges you should be aware of:

> **iROI-Mindchange 1:** „For those, who do not define goals, all the ways are impossible…" We need to define new goals because the world has changed!

- 85% of all Internet users find their specific websites by search engines.

- 90% of all Internet users look at the most 30 resulting links of the results of search engines only.

- 75% of all Internet users who use search engines have the intention to purchase an item or service.

Digital Mindchanges for CEOs
Dear CEO!

As a matter of fact there is no enterprise that succeeds in winning new customers 100% only by the using the internet - though it might have been promised to you many times. Even AMAZON has printed marketing material it sends to households! Today iROI Strategic Internet Marketing will enable you to understand how to gain new customers by using internet marketing and social media in addition to your traditional marketing.

We are very proud to be the original Internet Marketing Strategy that has helped so many businesses find their successful ways in digital times!

The iROI-Internet-Marketing-Strategy supports each CEO to establish profitable Internet Marketing - no matter to which specific field your business may belong. **We have more than 500 Testimonals on our website sauldie.org from all kinds of businesses profiting from our special knowledge.** And in case you do have a specific problem or question about gaining new customers in your specific field over the Internet, let me and my team know!

I am sure we will be able to serve you with innovative ideas that might give your business a positive kick to gain new customers. For sure it will be my pleasure to receive your questions via mail, phone or direct contact. At this point, let me wish you a lot of success in reaching your goals! Enjoy!

Sincerely yours,

Sanjay Sauldie
Creator of the iROI®-Internet Marketing Strategy

Any questions? Ask us anything you like!

„Not to believe, not to know and not to understand does not mean to be protected from new innovations."

Sanjay Sauldie

Digital Mindchanges for CEOs
Table of content

Digital Mindchanges for CEOs 6

    Dear CEO! 6

    Table of content 9

    Introduction 12

    The prosumers 15

    The audience is selecting 16

    Knowledge is power – no, it is not! 17

    time is money – not really! 17

    People are looking for jobs, cars, house and status – untrue! 18

Web 0.X: Conservative approach 19

    You cannot win 2015 with the rules of 1990 19

    Customer chooses his channel 20

    Customer Touch Points 20

    Change of Gadgets – change of Marketing Rules 21

    The customer journey 22

    Customer expects Brand Engagement 22

Web 1.0: Conversion 24

    Website = Sales Person 24

    Responsive design 25

Any questions? Ask us anything you like!

Analyze your webpage for free 29

Google dance 31

A glance at the iROI-Strategy 31

Summary: 34

Web 2.0: Conversation **35**

Conversation is everywhere 35

Social Web Marketing 36

Social media effect 36

Big Data, Smart Data 38

Social Boards 40

Social Media Reputation-Mangement 41

Create buzz 41

satisfaction effect 42

Social Media Marketing is permission based 43

Facebook 43

Never buy fans 45

Attention is the new Money 46

Social Media rules 48

Attraction economy 51

internet return on involvement 51

Digital Mindchanges for CEOs
Table of content

    economy of attraction 52

    Customer engagement 52

    automatic marketing 53

    Automatic: My simple digital world 55

    Social Media Policy 56

    sharing economy 57

    Social Media Ethics 57

    social media plan 58

Web 3.0: Confidence 61

    Open Innovation 61

    innovation speed 63

Web 4.0: Continuity: internet of things 66

Appendix 68

    Search engine optimization checklist 68

    Thank you so much! 72

    we support snehalaya 73

    we support SOS-Kinderdörfer 74

Bye bye, dear reader – stay conected! 75

    Book Sanjay Sauldie as speaker or as coach 76

Any questions? Ask us anything you like!

Digital Mindchanges for CEOs

Dear CEO,

twenty years ago I studied mathematics and informatics at the Cologne University, Germany, and to finance my studies I used to sell computer cables at a big store.

You know, these cables connected a computer with the World Wide Web and in twenty years this cable has changed the way we live, the way we communicate and the way we do business. Now the main question is: How can we use the potential of this cable for business? In this book we want to talk about how this cable is changing our world and what we have to know to be prepared for the changes that are hitting our business.

Introduction

We are in the middle of a big evolution, a digital revolution. What does that mean? The good news of every evolution is, that new animals, new systems and new markets develop. The bad news of an evolution is that animals, businesses, markets vanish! In today's world dinosaurs have no chance to survive, they had their chance and are lost forever. Companies have to be aware of, what evolution is doing to their businesses, doing to their customers! How is the customer behaviour changing and what do we have to know and do, to be prepared for it? We started on four feet running through the jungles, we developed through hunting, civilization, industry, information ages, then we entered the knowledge age. And we are now at the verge of virtuality and digitalization age.

And the main news I can give you today is:

> **iROI-Mindchange 2:** All markets have changed, whether you want it or not, and whether you believe it or not.

A radical change has occurred in the world of advertising and marketing and today only those businesses will survive which can adapt best to the changes internet has started.

Do you know what is happening in 60 seconds in the world? 600 new YouTube videos are being uploaded. You know, that is so much stuff in 60 seconds that you need a day to watch the whole program of what has been uploaded!

186 million e-mails are being sent, luckily we don't have to read them all. The world is changing at a speed that only companies, which understand how this whole new world functions and adapt their business to these new changes, will survive, and the others will have to face a lot of difficulties.

In Germany, we have many companies which have already lost market shares and even dissolved themselves forever, ex. g. Schlecker, Quelle, Praktiker, although they were leading companies once! It is a big change and it is affecting national and international companies at a very high scale.

695 thousand Facebook status updates per minute, who are these people, who have the time and why are they spending time at this place? And how can we use them to market our products, how can **we make use of 60 seconds** which is changing the whole industrial world?

Any questions? Ask us anything you like!

And it is affecting your industry at a very big scale. We'll see examples, so that you can see how and why this is not just a trend, it is part of a larger change today.

> **iROI-Mindchange 3:** The three main points for success in digital times are: you have to attract, engage and excite people.

We are overwhelmed by all the communication that is hitting us, print advertising, television, radio, all these channels. And do you know what the customer is doing?

He is thinking about which channels to use! To make him involved with your products, you have to attract, engage and excite him everywhere. The people want that!

> **iROI-Mindchange 4:** Even if we don't want the internet, the customer uses it and if we want to sell to this customer, we have to alter our business in a way that the customer likes.

He loves to become a fan, he enjoys being an evangelist for our products, for our brand – or he leaves us and goes to a brand that delivers this good feeling. The customer loyalty has changed – also Nokia (once the world market leader in mobile phones) had to experience that! Where is Nokia today? Do you see what evolution does to companies that do not adapt the change?

> **iROI-Mindchange 5:** The customers have stopped listening to what we are sending to them, the customers have started choosing what to listen to.

When you go to an airport, when you go to a train-station, when you are standing anywhere in this new world, you see people with mobile phones! They don't want to receive interruptive marketing, that is an old marketing method. Interruptive marketing had its day. Ask television channels – what problems they are having to get advertisement for their interruptive marketing – ask newspapers why the ads are getting lesser and lesser. They all have one thing in common:

> **iROI-Mindchange 6:** We are at a place in a time where all the marketing standards have changed and we have to learn – it's LEARN OR PERISH!

The prosumers

The prosumers (**pro**ducers and customer**s**) have started creating content themselves. Everybody using products has started blogging, everybody who has an opinion has started blogging, and they do it without getting money for it, they do it because of their own motivation.

We have to tell the world something about us, something about the products we use. It will be part of our marketing strategy to use this power to multiply our brand's messages. We must invite our target group to listen to our brand and products!

The audience is selecting

The times are over when people used to sit in front of the television and say: "Oh it's eight o'clock it's time for the news." We have a mobile device and everyone has access to all the world news when he wants, where he wants and he can even chose the source. The choice is very big. This change gives the digital remote control into the hands of the customer. In earlier times we could send a lot of information, but is was very, very difficult, to connect with customers. Here the internet has done a great job:

> **iROI-Mindchange 7:** In the history of mankind it has never been so easy to connect to your customer!

It is less than 5% of all businesses in the world which are capable of understanding this change and profiting from it. 95% are wasting money and they don't know for what! They are losing time and they don't know why! We have to join hands! We have the methods and must use them wisely and intelligently. If you ask these 5% of successful businesses, what is your secret? This is the answer:

> **iROI-Mindchange 8:** We must unlearn what we have learned!

Can you imagine, what that means for marketing? I'll show three things that have changed!

Knowledge is power – no, it is not!

In today's world, the world's knowledge can be goggled, it is in Google. You just type in anything you want to know about. Knowledge is freely accessible everywhere at every point, at any time: you can just access any information you want.

So knowledge can't be power, that has changed, a mindchange has happened.

> **iROI-Mindchange 9:** Applied knowledge is success! You have to know what you are doing and why! Albert Einstein already said: "…any fool can know, the point is, to understand…"

Then, there is another old mindset:

time is money – not really!

You must have heard that very often, also here the world has changed:

> **iROI-Mindchange 10:** Time is priceless.

Investing money gains you time, but you can't send me a second back into my past life! Every second you are losing is gone forever! Your competitor is maybe using time wisely!

Nothing in life is to be feared. Those who learn, adapt to the new world and lead – the rest are not interesting for mankind!

Any questions? Ask us anything you like!

People are looking for jobs, cars, house and status – untrue!

> **iROI-Mindchange 11:** People are looking for 3 things in today's time: recognition, attention and being a star for 30 seconds.

This is the reason why people love Facebook and other social networks. Posting a selfie and someone likes it – wow what a great attention. Someone even comments – thank you for your recognition! And if then someone watches their video on Youtube - then they are a star for 30 seconds! If we know these motivators, we should be using them for the promotion of our sales! If you see what is happening in 60 seconds, sometimes you may think, oh my God, what is happening there, must I fear it? No, not at all.

> **iROI-Mindchange 12:** Nothing in life is to be feared, it is only to be understood. Now is the time to understand more, so that we may fear less.

This is not a sentence of today's world, this is a quote from Mary Curie in 1897!

If we want to be successful in business, we have to start learning and never stop again. That's the main thing we have to know, because the markets have changed and what we are going to do is now, we are going to enter the web world, Web 0.X, that's a conservative approach to Internet and we are going to reach Web 4.0. **Welcome back to school!**

Web 0.X: Conservative approach

So, what does web 0.X mean? In the 1980s, you could reach more people with 0.X. Why? Because the variety of choice of media was not big. The media used to have undivided attention.

You cannot win 2015 with the rules of 1990

In 2015 the world has changed, more media reaches fewer people, because they are paying less attention. You know, even in my seminars, there are some who are using their iPads, their iPhones. But that is normal.

Our attention is diverted very easily, because we have the choice of media. If we do marketing, then it's not enough to be sending one signal through one channel. What we have to do is: send all information into all channels, because we don't know (nobody does!), which channel the customer is using at the moment and in the future.

Never do marketing only in one channel and hope, that will give you a lot of customers – you are loosing them elsewhere. What we have to do, we have to join different media into one strategy. The awareness of a customer is sinking! We have to get the awareness for our brand, for our products, for what we stand for, from every channel!

We are facing a change in the mass media. Here are some figures from the US only: in 1960 they had 4.400 radio stations and today there are 13.000, in 1960 there were 8.400 magazines, today 17.300 want to reach the readers!

Can you imagine what that means for the customer? So much choice, so many channels and then of course, millions of sites, billions of pages on the internet!

Customer chooses his channel

The customer has opened his channels using new devices.

> **iROI-Mindchange 13:** The way information is being spread, is changing at a lightning speed. And a brand has to be visible on every gadget that is on the market. Otherwise it is losing a new market place where another brand will come and become visible to these customers.

Now, let us see what an online customer does in his normal life.

Customer Touch Points

The customer is reading a friend's posting on Facebook, visiting blogs, buying tickets online for movies, even going to gaming sites! There are statistics in Germany, that tell there are more women playing online games than men. World of Warcraft, who knows World of Warcraft? **Ask your children!**

They know more about it than we, because they are using it daily. There may be psychological or social reasons behind that. I don't want to talk about, what the men are doing, why the women are playing games instead of playing with their husbands and vice versa, but that's another question.

Comparison portals are growing at a great speed! The customer compares products and services and gets the best price! Sports and fitness sites are growing at a massive speed, because more and more people, more and more customers want to cocoon at home, they want to stay at home, but they want all the information they need.

Change of Gadgets – change of Marketing Rules

It's unbelievable but it's happening. Air Berlin in Germany has started a new system where you can access special programs with your iPad when you are on the aeroplane. You can hear music, you can see nice pictures, so that you don't think of any fear of flying or anything else.

> **iROI-Mindchange 14:** Our gadgets have changed and what we need to do is, we have to understand customer touch points! Where does a customer get into touch with our products, how can we be visible there and how can we ensure that all channels are being used in a strategic way and not used just by chance?

Think about it! Often I hear from CEOs: Let's make a Facebook fan page and hope something will happen. But often nothing really happens – that is not the right way to face Social Media in today's digital times!

> **iROI-Mindchange 15:** Hope is good, strategy is better.

You are spending money, you are spending time, do something sensible with it! In these digital worlds you have to have an internet marketing strategy behind the brand and behind your efforts.

The customer journey

We have to make unaware people aware of what good quality we deliver, what perfect products we have, and then the customer journey begins.

After getting to know our products, the customer tries and tests our products, after trying he uses it, after using he sometimes uses it regularly and then uses it exclusively.

This customer journey is not linear today as in the old days. Today the customer journey is completely nonlinear. He has a choice, he goes to Twitter, he gets information, he engages, he ask questions, he goes to a place to purchase or to compare prices, gets aware, tells his friends, asks his friends, discusses it. And wants to engage with us!

Customer expects Brand Engagement

We found out, that the customer is well informed (sometimes even better informed than the sales staff at the store!), he knows what we are doing and if he gets to know what we are doing, how we are doing, he is also sharing it with the rest of the world. Not only in his small circle of friends, where he is telling, oh, I'm using this, that's only the first part of mouth to mouth marketing. But the main thing that is changing is: he is telling it to the whole world.

Web 0.X: Conservative approach
Customer expects Brand Engagement

And what happens, if he is disappointed, what happens then? He doesn't go into his room, starts weeping in a corner, and says, oh I bought something, I'm so sad.

You know what he does? He uses the internet, he tells the whole world, if his experience with the product was good, if his shopping experience was good, if the use of the products was good for him or not. So what we have to understand is, this world has become more transparent and wide open!

We are now entering the world called Web 1.0. What is Web 1.0?

Web 1.0: Conversion

Web 1.0 is the world of Internet marketing, marketing through your website. But if you talk to the 5% of successful businesses, you know what they answer? "We do not have a website anymore."

If you talk to Amazon, if you talk to eBay, if you talk to any of those companies who are really, really successful in the web, especially also in Web 1.0, they all say: "We do not have a website anymore."

Can you imagine Amazon not having a website anymore? So when you ask them: "You are telling me that you don't have a website, so what is that at www.amazon.com?"

> **iROI-Mindchange 16:** They told me to uncover a big secret: Successful businesses in Internet do not have a website anymore, they have engaged a new sales person online!

This sales person has certain capabilities. Can you imagine that you have a worker in your company with sleeping defects, a worker in your company who doesn't sleep at night, who works 24 hours for you?

Website = Sales Person

Can you imagine having a worker in your business, who has no friends, who works 7 days a week for you? Can you imagine having a worker in your company who never gets sick? This is, what these companies have understood:

> **iROI-Mindchange 17:** We do not have a technical solution: a website – we have a digital sales person!

They have a new sales lady. She never gets sick, she works 24 hours a day without getting tired, she is never on vacation and she works 7 days a week every day without getting tired.

The only thing that has changed is, she has a new make-up, a new shape and design. She doesn't look like a traditional sales woman, she wears a new outfit, she has a new presence – she is digitally empowered! She appears on screens and looks perfect on every screen.

Responsive design

Your website has to automatically adjust its content to the resolution of every gadget. And I am not talking about reducing your font size to arial 3 – that no one can read! You need a responsive design so that your website – your beautiful lady must communicate perfectly on every gadget!

> **iROI-Mindchange 18:** We don't need a website, we need a sales person in the internet who is selling for us, who is doing marketing for us, who is providing our contacts to new customers, who is taking care, that we are staying in business and growing in our business.

Any questions? Ask us anything you like!

So, there are two parts in building a website, one way is you build a website that is beautiful, that is what 95% do, they have beautiful websites. Do you think that the website of Amazon is beautiful? eBay is also not very beautiful, but why do these companies, who have so much money, why don't they build beautiful websites?

They want to sell!

> **iROI-Mindchange 19:** For selling you need intelligence and that's the difference: this sales lady can be very beautiful, but if she is not intelligent, she won't sell a thing.

We need a beautiful **and** intelligent website. And what does intelligence mean? Now, beauty is relative, we can talk days and nights over it and think about, what is beauty.

I know professors who spend months and months making designs for our customers, waisting time and money on both sides – the design in the internet does not need to be reinvented – we just have to follow the rules of the successful websites – that's all!

> **iROI-Mindchange 20:** Forget this old stuff of designing till death – start optimizing for sales now!

So what we should do is, follow what successful companies are doing, they are concentrating on the website intelligence.

Web 1.0: Conversion
Responsive design

Can you imagine that big companies like Daimler Benz, Nestlé, General Motors also have a sales woman on the web and a major part of their success still depends on Google?

> **iROI-Mindchange 21:** The problem of this young Google is: he is blind because he has no human eyes!

He has no eyes, so you can have the most beautiful sales lady on the web: if he doesn't like her, you are dead!

> **iROI-Mindchange 22:** If Google doesn't like your website – he will not recommend your products!

Google is not a search engine, that's very often misinterpreted! Google is doing something very important for us: marketing! Type a word into Google, maybe MASCARA. Then Google shows you aprroximately 81 million sales ladies on the web he found. Oh my God!

From these 81 million results, he found out in 0.25 seconds, he makes a list. He shows the customer this list. When you are searching something, do you look at the first page, the first search results?

At our academy we do a lot of research on this topic: the first page, the first ten search results are watched by 100%, the second page only by 50%, the third page under 20%, fourth page under 5% and after the fifth page only 0.x% people watch. What does that mean for our business?

> **iROI-Mindchange 23:** If we are not in the top 50 of Google, then we can have the most beautiful website in the world, it won't gain us any new customers. If you are not in the top 10 list with your keywords, you are losing customers!

We would be gaining only customers who already know our brand name, already know what we are selling! That is a nice thing to have, but what we want are new, fresh customers who are ready to join our brand and buy our products!

> **iROI-Mindchange 24:** Intelligent websites understand and follow the rules of search engines!

There are rules, and these are not design rules, these are rules in programming, rules of strategy: how to get that customer, a unknown customer on the website to be identified?

And that is the job of this sales woman: she has to take care how many people are visiting your website and how many of them are getting into contact with you. That is called the **internet return on invest (iROI)** of a website.

Some CEOs say: We've got 10.000 visitors a day. Cool, isn't it? We are satisfied! You know how you can get that very easily? Put a picture of Britney Spears on to your homepage, take care that you've got the legal rights on the pictures, and then you have visitors, but none of them is a real potential customer!

Web 1.0: Conversion
Analyze your webpage for free

So, what we need to measure is not the number of the visitors, it is the number of the **contacts per visitor**. Then you know how healthy your sales women in the web is, it is called the internet return on invest. Increase it!

> **iROI-Mindchange 25:** Every cent that you invest, every minute, every second has to gain you contacts.

If you have 100.000 visitors and less buyers, then you have a problem!

> **iROI-Mindchange 26:** It can be sometimes wiser for businesses to have less visitors, but the right visitors.

Those visitors, who are already interested, who don't need to be persuaded, who are already fans, who love you and who recommend you and then multiplicate your advertising material, your advertising slogan, everything that you put in this channel: they already know you and where to find you. It is about new customers, who do not know, that you exist!

The main thing what we need is an IROI, don't measure only how many visitors you have, you have to measure the contacts per visitor!

Analyze your webpage for free

To analyze your website, what you have to do is, you have to find easy tools. One of these tools is called **SEO (search engine optimization) doctor,** this you get free in the internet, it integrates as an extension to your Firefox browser.

Any questions? Ask us anything you like!

Just Google it, just type into Google "SEO doctor Firefox".

It is for business people like us who are not interested in programming, but want to know if our sales lady is doing well or not!

It adds a flag in the browser, and if you click on this flag, it shows you, what you need to do to improve your website for search engines. Now the nice thing is, we don't need to do it ourselves! Just talk to your web designer, talk to your web company and ask them to consider this valuable information.

What we always have to do is, while designing a website, we have to always take care of two target groups. One target group is our customer, a human being with eyes and feelings. That's why it has to be emotional, beautiful, but we should never forget that there is a second person who is important, too, who is also looking at our website, that is Google.

I've given you a plan (see Appendix), how to develop a website, how to develop a clean strategy, so that you are not only taking care of the beauty, but also taking care of the inner strength, the intelligence of this sales person. And if you would employ a real sales lady today, then you will not only be looking at the beauty, you would also be motivating her to learn, to go to courses! And that is the same thing we have to do, when we are talking about our website. You have to understand the Google algorithm and then implement this knowledge and make your website intelligent for search engines. Because a search engine is nothing else than a piece of software, not more, there is no human being sitting there, watching your beautiful website!

Google doesn't even know what a brand is. That's why in the top ten you often don't include big brands, but blogs and content that is more relevant!

> **iROI-Mindchange 27:** Google is not brand aware, Google is intelligence and relevance aware.

Google from time to time updates its criteria to clean up the search engine results. It is called…

Google dance

Google does a very simple thing: When too many companies are optimizing their websites, then many websites may be very similar. When google started, if you wrote a good text on your website, your website-ranking went up easily. When suddenly more than 10 Websites had relevant text, Google needed new criteria. It introduced pictures. So it went on – today we figure out more than 80 things google and other search engines are looking at. See the appendix for the complete list!

A glance at the iROI-Strategy

Step 1: How good is your website prepared for customers?

At this point analyze your current website. It is going to be your target group which is going to visit this website and it depends upto them how many times they will come back to your website to turn into your customer. Test the programming code now at http://validator.w3.org

Any questions? Ask us anything you like!

Step 2: Are you optimizing for your target group?

To improve your Internet Marketing efforts we can help you to activate your target group to visit your website. Therefore your turnover per visitor will be improved as a result. In this step we help you define the right target group(s) for whom your website should be optimized.

Step 3: Have you really chosen the right keywords?

Well chosen keywords are the secret of your website's success. We will support you in finding the right keywords the customers are really looking for. It doesn't make sense to optimize your web for keyphrases that nobody uses. Did you ever check which phrases are really being used by interested customers? We do that together with you!

Step 4: Let´s optimize your website now!

The optimization of your website for search engines is very important, so that your customers are able to find your business among the top rankings of the search results.

We shall enable you to optimize your website for search engines and to learn how search engines function at all. Eliminate the mistakes found in Step 1 to 3 and incorporate the corrections on your web.

We teach you and your team how to do it so that you are not depending on us forever – we like to give freedom to our customers!

Step 5: Is your Internet Marketing integrated?

To find somebody who is able to create a brochure or a website for you is going to be easy. But what sense does a nice brochure have if it does not get to your potential customers? Therefore this step should help to analyze your marketing. Only consequent marketing will attract the attention of your potential customers in the end.

Step 6: What are visitors doing on your page?

At this point we shall have a look at website statistics. We shall see your website's statistics before and after its optimization. You will always see an improvement between the website visitors and the generated turnover. We are very well specialized in this field and will enable you to implement the necessary statistical software to your business too.

Step 7: Strategic positioning

Within this last step we take care that your business receives the correct positioning and is found in portals, chat rooms and so on. Also the use of new technology (Blogs, iPodding, Videoblogging) is implemented and we can develop your future in the web.

Summary:

Always pay attention to the effect of your individual web-design, because it is leading to visitors and search engine result lists. If you follow the above mentioned suggestions you will increase the chances for the success for your Internet business.

Actually, we could answer many more of the exciting questions about the Internet Marketing for you.

- Where does your website stand in search engines?
- What do your competitors do better than you?
- How do search engines see your website?
- How well is the structure and design of your website?
- How many programming mistakes are within the code of your website?
- Which keywords are used in connection to your field?
- How can you find out most wanted searching keywords?
- Which websites should cooperate with yours?
- Who finds the most suitable strategic partners?
- How fascinating is your specific subject presented to your customers?
- How is your position developing in search engines?
- Who signs you up for the most important portals?

Web 2.0: Conversation

In earlier times a customer bought a product, found it good or bad and there the communication ended, he had paid and left the store, very good for us, we had what we wanted!

Now the customers are talking about you everywhere, they are talking about your brand, they are talking about your behavior, they are talking about the behavior at the point of sale, they are talking about the experience they are having with your product and the important thing is:

> **iROI-Mindchange 28:** Web 2.0, social web, doesn't care if you like it or not – it just exists and works with or without you (remember this page whenever you listen to U2 playing this song!)!

Web 2.0 is this whole world of wikis, recommendations, audio, videos etc. but this is a world which is changing our whole marketing again, 180 degrees change, because the customer has changed his habits.

Conversation is everywhere

More and more of your customers are twenty-four hours online! Before we enter world web 2.0 marketing, we have to understand the dark side of web 2.0. You know what the dark side is? The problem is, many companies just go blindly into social web, because they had heard from somebody: "oh social web is important, okay let's also do something in social web." Would you do bungee-jumping without a rope?

Social Web Marketing

Social web has a dark side, and before doing anything in social web, we have to be aware of what is this dark side about. If we don't know the dark side it can be, that we just do all the mistakes, that other companies did and are doing, because they are not aware of the dark side.

People are talking about us, even if we are not active in social media, even if we don't do anything in social media, we are already present in the social media. This happened to Dell. Jeff Jarvis wrote on his blog that he is not satisfied with the customer care of Dell. Now everybody of us would say, okay, one customer who is not happy, okay, nothing will happen.

Something happened!

Jeff wrote in his blog that he is not satisfied: he invented a new buzz word, a new word, called Dell-Hell and wrote about it in his blog. Other people shared his experience, they multiplied his blog articles in their own blogs, because they had had the same experience with Dell! This reached Wall-Street and investors lost faith in Dell! Dell lost a lot of money – their shares fell because of one person: Jeff Jarvis! We call it

The Social media effect

This is the history of one message, one content created goes to blogs, smaller blogs, bigger blogs, it goes to Twitter, it goes to Facebook, multiplies and suddenly your story is in the top ten in the Google search engine. Somebody else could be writing about you and if we are not ready to understand the

Web 2.0: Conversation
The Social media effect

dark side, you will never know why suddenly your customers are not buying any more and disapperaring!

Customers are reading exactly these blogs, these Facebook pages, they are reading what Google is finding about the brand, they are getting all this information.

> **iROI-Mindchange 29:** If we close our eyes and shut our ears: it doesn't mean that messages are not being multiplied. We are only not part of the conversation!

We can't stop it, the only thing we can do is we can react through understanding. If we know what is happening, we can react on it. And there are many places, where we should know what is really happening. If we don't use and react on social media, then certain things happen out of our control.

Do you know the company Nestlé, it's a Swiss company. They have a product called Kit Kat. One person went on to the Nestle website and wrote: "Nestlé, you are using palm oil for producing chocolate and to get this oil rain forests are being destroyed." Now the social media manager at Nestlé must have thought, "Wir sind eine Schweizer Firma!", we are a Swiss company, we are so big, why is he disturbing our news? And then deleted this message!

Deleting this message led to a storm of blogs which wrote about Nestlé deleting a message and they spread this information in a shitstorm. Then a company came and said: "Let us do a real research on it!" and they did a research on it.

The company was Greenpeace. Now imagine, you are the brand manager of Kit Kat Nestlé, and suddenly you are seeing this video on youtube:

https://www.youtube.com/watch?v=ToGK3-2tZz8

Can you imagine that this had an effect on the sales of Nestlé, of Kit Kat? Only (!) 237.900 people watched this video.

> **iROI-Mindchange 30:** If we are not ready to learn and listen, we will have to feel!

Big Data, Smart Data

The most important thing in today's world of marketing is the data of the customer. That company, that person who has access to the data of a person, can send him marketing material fitting to his demands. Stop waisting marketing money by sending information to people who are not interesting for our marketing! Save money from being wasted!

> **iROI-Mindchange 31:** You could send your marketing material only to those persons who are interested in your products. And this is the strength! We are talking about the white side of social media: If this whole data is being stored, why shouldn't we use it?

What would happen if we would use it wisely, it's legal and the information is freely available!

Imagine you want to make a next deal with a business person, wouldn't it be nice to know what type of hobbies he has, what food he likes? And this is what people are doing, especially in the sales department! People go here: **Yasni.de** and **glassdoor.com** – they are free.

If you have children, then please sit down with your children, go to this page in your country and type in the name of your child, because the whole human resources departments of the companies now are using this as their starting page.

When a young person applies for a job, the first thing they do is, they put the name in **yasni.de** or **glassdoor.com**. Go and see! If there is something like, "I love drinking till I fall into coma" on the pages of your kids, they will have difficulties in getting jobs later when they grow up!

> **iROI-Mindchange 32:** We always have to think of two things: one thing, our private life! In our private life don't go into the social web, in business life, you must use all the possibilities for your business.

So we always have to think about two things, protect your privacy and use the information others are sending for your business success.

These are two worlds, these are two sides of the same coin, please take care of your own name, take care of your private life! In your private life call your friends, meet with them, you don't need to enter social media.

Any questions? Ask us anything you like!

> **iROI-Mindchange 33:** In business life you have to go and use social media, because your customers are there. We have to distinguish: are we talking about social media for our private life or are we talking about social media for our business, these are two completely different things.

My advice: In private you don't have time to go for Social Media and post "oh I'm sitting in a café and having a drink. " – how boring!

Don't do the mistake and make a picture of your Bang and Olufsen Stereo three dimensional super television and post it on Facebook and ten days later write in Facebook: "I'm going on vacation for fourteen days!" Your home could be cleaned up, when you return, because people are reading your posts – also thieves!

But one thing, you have to be in social media for business! And that's a very important decision: Whenever you write anything, either on the website or on your profile, be careful, it is being read thousand times. And yasni is a place where it is being collected forever!

Social Boards

For brands it is very important to know in which social boards people are talking about our products, because it is not enough to only rely on Google's search results for your company name. Google cannot enter any places where you need a login.

That's why there is a **boardreader.com**, that's a search engine for boards! It shows what information there is about you or about your brand.

Social Media Reputation-Mangement

A Google alert is a very helpful tool, you type in your search query into this field, for example, your name! Whenever Google finds anything connected to your name it will send you an e-mail.

> **iROI-Mindchange 34:** Companies and private people need a reputation management to check what people are talking about you. Set up an Google Alert now!

This makes your life easier: on the one hand, you don't have to look after it every day yourself, one the other hand you know, which website has material about you.

You can also put in a search query for all other companies who are selling the same products like you and you have an enemy watch – your own personal CIA!

Create buzz

Buzz is a new word in the social media marketing, buzz means, people talking about you, are you interesting for the public or are you just a boring brand like many, many others in the market? That's why many companies are creating new buzz!

Any questions? Ask us anything you like!

Addictomatic.com is a great tool to control buzz. It tells you, who is tweeting, who has a blog, who has a video in YouTube, which pictures in flicker are been uploaded, which wordpress.com information is there! This is very valuable for somebody doing marketing - based on your keyword you type in! Who is publishing pictures, who is sending video news!

> **iROI-Mindchange 35:** Today we have a complete dashboard for the control of social media!

To have good buzz, we need to do some homework!

The satisfaction effect

First we need to satisfy the customer, then they come again and again, become repeated customers, then they do a mouth to mouth marketing, they become an evangelist and sometimes they even become developers, that means, they start helping you develop new products.

We will talk about that later, because that is already the step to Web 3.0, but first we have to learn more about Web 2.0.

> **iROI-Mindchange 36:** The friends of my customers and customers are potential customers!

Next time you are in the office, take your database-list of customers and send them an e-mail: "Dear customer, we just understood that all your friends are potential customers for us, that's why we have an excel list in the attachment, please put all the names of your friends into this excel list and send

Web 2.0: Conversation
Social Media Marketing is permission based

it back, thank you for helping us doing marketing at your friends." How many e-mails will you get back?

Zero, we even talk about minus results, because somebody will sue you and say: "how can you use my friend's names to do marketing, this is illegal." They live in an old world!

Social Media Marketing is permission based

That's why somebody invented something for us business people. We have to go there to do business with the friends of our customers, because luckily our customers don't know what they are doing. This place has only been invented for business; it is not a place for having friends. If you want friends, you've got some good friends in your phonebook, call them, meet them, have a nice drink!

> **iROI-Mindchange 37:** In your private life you don't need 10.000 friends you don't even know.

But for marketing, how important would it be, if we could reach the friends of our customers with their permission? I call this place marketing heaven:

Facebook

I'm not there to get to know more people; I already know many. I'm there so that my marketing message is multiplied and I reach the friends of my customers! If a customer becomes a friend of yours or a fan, then something magical happens. My posts are being multiplied automatically through other users – so I save a lot of time and money on marketing!

Any questions? Ask us anything you like!

My comments on my facebook profile have only one intention: visibility and to get to know the friends of my customer and build my status as an expert! I have an Avatar profile for my private, really private world and for the business I have my business profile. I'm in Facebook to do business and if you go into Facebook, always have in mind: only for business.

I want as many people as possible to get the information I want to send, that's why, if someone wants to become my friend – **everyone is welcome**!

Thank you for giving me access to all your friends! In the second, when I click on "yes, friendship accepted", the magic happens! People get curious and want to know why someone liked me! You know why? It has nothing to do with Internet or with social media, it is human, we are a curious species!

> **iROI-Mindchange 38:** Social media is about relationship, you always build up a relationship, never think of selling!

With one message you'll send information to thousands of people. It is nothing else as we used to do! Do you remember radio spots? Maybe hundred thousand are listening, maybe five will react! For these five we did this whole marketing. In social media it is the same, not all people will react to your posts, but those who will, those are the important multipliers of your information – they will do the marketing for you!

Facebook is offering you their big data. You can put ads on Facebook that are matched to your key target group and only shown to people who belong to your target group. This Big Data is very detailed and can be used for a small amount of money at www.facebook.com/ads

Never buy fans

If your children suddenly get a cheque for about some hundred dollars, don't be worried, they may be working as fan slaves. You can buy fans! So if you have a friend and your friend says, oh, I want to have some fans, then you can send him a Christmas gift, for example you can send him plenty thousand real fans for 999 Euros, and overnight he will have 20.000 fans, it's good for the ego, for marketing in business life: forget it.

> **iROI-Mindchange 39:** You don't need **many fans**, you need the **right fans**, those who are evangelists, who love you and multiply your information.

If you have got the right people, the fans will take care, that the number of your fans grows with others who really love you. And even if somebody posts something negative about you, your fans will help you.

> **iROI-Mindchange 40:** Don't get fake friends – they never help – neither in real life, nor in digital life!

Always remember, we are in times where multiplication has become very, very important. What you will need is someone to answer questions: a social media marketing manager! If somebody asks questions in the Social Web, there has to be someone to answer them, and that is very important, because people are expecting it.

Attention is the new currency

We have reached the age where we have to communicate with our customers, otherwise they will communicate at places like yasni, where we cannot control it! In Social Media we can control it, we can respond to it, we can react on it!

> **iROI-Mindchange 41:** We are talking about care! Your information is being evaluated. What's the most important thing in digital times? Attention! Please give human beings attention – they will love you for that!

You have got the most relevant relationship in your life, because attention cannot be bought. And here in Facebook it's the first time that we can have direct contact with our customers, we can talk to them, we can find out what they like and what they don't like, we can start talking with them, giving them attention and respect, because they are those who are financing our lifes.

They are not some idiots who are just buying our products and not doing anything else. They love us! If we can multiply our fans, if we can make fans to our sales person, imagine what it could change in your industry! That's why do one thing: setup a fan page and tell every visitor on your website, that you have a fan page and let them like your fan page.

Web 2.0: Conversation
Attention is the new currency

We don't know how many people are visiting your website just at this moment and they have no chance to become fans of you, because the button, "like me on Facebook" may be missing.

So if you post anything, people can get to know what you are doing, so be very careful before posting any information into the web, because it is forever there, it will never be taken out.

You can increase your fans on the one hand through your existing fans already, telling them that they should tell this to their friends, or competition games, or you can also have a social attachment and say, "help us get 5.000 fans! As soon as we get the 5.000 fans we will donate 1.000 dollars for a welfare organisation or just for welfare."

> **iROI-Mindchange 42:** Make it a social story. Not a marketing campaign!

Why should someone become a fan? Either one already is an existing fan, because one knows your product or if one doesn't know you, then you have to make a good impression! It's the same with human beings. So, if you leave a good impression on the web, show it on to your Facebook! It's a perfect thing, it works, because people say, I can do something for free, becoming a friend and then the company will do something sensible. It's great for social branding, it's really brand optimization in social media. Give them something special, give them the newest product tips for free, motivate them to do something! They will love it - and your company!

Any questions? Ask us anything you like!

> **iROI-Mindchange 43:** You must develop a culture of how human beings can be reached with very simple methods!

These are not complicated things, to program something like this is really not big deal. We develop such ideas with companies with great success!

Remember, we always are talking about the social media effect! What if we were sending the content and it gets multiplied to all these channels, instead of always being fearful, "oh, I hope nobody wrote something bad about me"?

Do not be fearful – not knowing, that's what you should be afraid of!

> **iROI-Mindchange 44:** Write so much good about you, that even if there is something bad about you, it becomes worthless!

It only works if everyone follows an integrated system of rules in your company: what is to be done, what is to be multiplied, of course YOU have to decide, what is to be done, when is it to be done and how is it to be done.

Social Media rules

But please follow own social media guidelines, that's the rule what you need for everything that is being done in the social web. Otherwise also bad things can happen.

Web 2.0: Conversation
Social Media rules

> **iROI-Mindchange 45:** Don't involve private things! Nobody in the world, if he is talking about your brand, has to know personal information! That always belongs to your private, private, private, private profile, really, very far away from anything doing with business!

Please make a real cut in your information policy and I can really advise you, it is very important first of all for your own sake, because all the information you are publishing is connected with all your profile information.

> **iROI-Mindchange 46:** News, political news has nothing to do on your brand page, your brand is always internationally neutral!

If you are not sure, if the information you want to publish, fits to the company's brand strategy then do not publish it!

> **iROI-Mindchange 47:** We are talking about really brutal times where anything you publish can be multiplied thousand times – and arouse reaction instantly (even on weekends or when you are sleeping!)

That's why, always plant the seeds, please, it is very important that you plant the seeds, let the plant grow, but take care that it is built on solid knowledge, on solid content, on solid news, solid information! Only then it will succeed on the long-term. It's very important that your social media manager is not from the old world, it has to be someone who loves Social Media and is always on with pleasure!

> **iROI-Mindchange 48:** For every 10.000 fans you need one social media marketing manager.

If you have 50.000 fans, you will need five Social Media Marketing Managers to answer all the questions, because we are talking about a real big number of people who want to listen calmly, but many of them are asking questions and expecting quick responses!

The best thing you can do is, go to schools and put a poster there that says: "We are looking for social media marketing managers!"

You can teach somebody how your business works, but you can't teach somebody, who is not used to being 24 hours on, to be 24 hours on.

> **iROI-Mindchange 49:** So you have to take someone who is already 24 hours on and teach him about your products, teach him about what social media really is, because these young people normally just have a vague notion about what **social media marketing** really is! It is different than just being on and posting selfies!

So, teach them and give them the chance to grow and they will be good friends, they will be really good friends to you. They will also give you new ideas!

We can help educate your team to perfect social media marketing managers!

Attraction economy

Our normal attention economy is based on interruption. The next time you see a film on the television, then you know what interruption means, okay, that is interruption marketing. Today it is engagement, people want to get engaged with you and they do it in their free time.

internet return on involvement

The world of return on investment has changed, too. We were talking about the website. Web 1.0 then meant return on investment and now we have reached a stage where one thing will be very important, the return on **involvement**.

Do you reach your target group, does the target group reach you, do you connect with them, do they connect with you, and do you like you?

You can build completely new brands, that will crash old brands, because old businesses are only counting on return on investment!

> **iROI-Mindchange 50:** "If I have a fan page, how much do I have to invest and how much will I get back?", that's the wrong approach – often told by CEOs who were controllers before!

What you need to know is: How many people will I get on to my fan page, how will I get involved with them, how will I take care that they multiply my message?

Any questions? Ask us anything you like!

economy of attraction

You don't need jobless heavy users, you need inspirational customers who are ready to carry your brand to their friends! Who love you, because your brand is great!

Customer engagement

What would happen, if we could ask our customer what type of product he would like to have? What would happen, if we could ask our customer:

"Hey, help us in product development, help us in product innovation, help us to improve our product portfolio. Which product do you love, which products do you need in different colors, which is the color of the month?"

You could engage them with your product with great success with least investment, and profit from it!

iROI-Mindchange 51:	PR 2.0 is Twitter

If you want to know how to join your website intelligently with Facebook, Twitter and LinkedIn, there is a place called **Twitterfeed.com**, and Twitter feed is a free tool that can feed your blog into Twitter, Facebook, LinkedIn and more.

You can connect it, but you need RSS technology on your website for it. You write something into your blog and it is automatically posted in Facebook, Twitter, and LinkedIn and so on.

automatic marketing

So we have reached the next step in the evolution of marketing, how much can we do automatically?

Old school approach: Let's write something and then write something in Facebook, write something for Twitter, that's a lot of work. So, also here the evolution has found a solution: Twitterfeed does it automatically! Multiply your content to all these social media places.

Beware of what you are posting. People will react and if somebody posts a question, then you have to react to it.

So it is not only a one way communication! People will ask questions and expect answers!

> **iROI-Mindchange 52:** Ask questions in your posts! Just do not send product information to the social web – that is boring!

How do you like our packaging, how did you find our product, where did you find our product? Just make people engaged with the product, they will like it, they will love it.

> **iROI-Mindchange 53:** You know, how often I correct my sentence while writing on the social web? The next generation says: "hey, just post it, gone and over, it's okay."

It's a different mentality, we have to adjust to it! When we post something it has to be grammatically perfect, no doubt, but we have to accept that those people who are writing may themselves have grammar problems.

No problem, as long as they buy our product. Okay, don't forget that!

If you are bombarding them every day, then they get bored, the attention is not there.

> **iROI-Mindchange 54:** It is better to write a post, when you have something interesting to tell!

So, better think one day more about what you are going to write and what effect it will have and then you can increase the buzz on the market. Buzz is how many reactions come to your post.

Always think that when you are posting, when you are already writing into your blog, then this information could be going automatically to the social media. Normally what you are writing in your blog is not really optimized for social sharing and so on.

You should have a plan. We advise our clients to have a monthly plan. Which product will be marketed and when, on the social web.

With this plan you have the security that you are sending information that is controlled and planned and you are not posting anything uncontrolled!

Automatic: My simple digital world

I'm traveling quite a lot as a speaker, so I sat down on a weekend and wrote 50 articles for the social web and then put them into my blog with a time schedule. When I'm traveling now, it could be that just then there is new blog post being multiplied to Facebook and so on, although I'm not even online! I'm in my plan. My sales lady is wise!

> **iROI-Mindchange 55:** You have a plan and these posts you write into your blog, they have a strategic sequence.

These are very deep ways on how to control all your data. You don't have to write every day, but you can write once, sit down and get your posts as you want to have them in the sequence you want to publish them! One post could be introducing a product, the second post could be doing marketing: "you get a special offer now if you buy in the next two hours."

This sequential development: that's the intelligence again of the website. This completely goes into the social web.

> **iROI-Mindchange 56:** Building up this plan, that's the real gold. If you do not have that – good luck!

If you have developed that, then you know which product is going to be promoted when! You now only need followers, you need fans which take your idea or brand or product and multiply it so that everybody can talk about it.

Any questions? Ask us anything you like!

iROI-Mindchange 57: The principle of social media is not really new! It's a digital way of mouth-to-mouth propaganda!

If Jesus would be living today He would be tweeting, 100%, because it's the new way of getting connnected to people.

iROI-Mindchange 58: Jesus was connected with Peter, John, Matthew and Andrew. They were all his evangelists, and that is what we need for our brand.

You only need twelve good fans, remember it, it already functioned once!

Social Media Policy

When we are talking about social media policy, do protect intellectual property! Avoid dangerous material, that is, don't talk about politics, religion, everything you wouldn't talk to a stranger! Don't post it.

Then do include industry specific guidelines, that's also very important. Talk about your industry, post new statistics about your products, inform your customers about it, don't hide this valuable information!

Give it away, spread it, tell the people that you are the expert, you are not only producing a product, but you are watching the market – and this will raise your digital reputation! Show the world that you are completely updated – and a reliable source of information!

Web 2.0: Conversation
sharing economy

Be part of the new...

sharing economy

That gives reliability, it gives you competence, and people rely on you and get the information from you. Then, do avoid conflicts of interests that could be through personal attachments like soccer, because somebody is a fan of Inter Mailand and the other is a fan of Juventus Turin and if you are now writing something positive about one soccer team, then you will have trouble with the others. So, keep neutral, provide and require clear disclaimers, that's very important! Especially in Germany the law is very strict about legal disclaimers. If you have a Facebook profile or a fan page, then you need legal disclaimers, otherwise other people can put you into legal trouble!

> **iROI-Mindchange 59:** Stay legal, that's legal stuff. I'm not a specialist on this legal stuff, but you have to have an exact definition about who is responsible for the disclaimer, who is responsible for the website, for the fan page and so on.

Social Media Ethics

You know this is an ethical question and we always advise that it is better to be ethically correct. In these times no one can really hide anything for long, because we have reached the stage where people are talking about everything and whistleblowers are everywhere. Also maybe in your company – be careful, not fearful! Go to **glassdoor.com** and check it!

If we follow ethical guidelines, we are showing the world, hey, we maybe not be the number one in the world, or we are on the way, or we want to stay the number one in the world, but we also have ethical guidelines and we respect third parties interests!

We don't ignore them, we do not move aggressively on the markets, but if we are ethically correct on the market, people will support us and help us!

> **iROI-Mindchange 60:** If you have employees who can access the fan page, it is important to make sure that they know your ethical standards, that they know what they are doing and why they are doing it.

If it is you alone, who is posting, that's okay, but if somebody else also has the right to post, talk about these problems, because sometimes a worker or somebody like an associate starts publishing things with bad consequences!

That does not mean you have to verify every post – that would contradict the freedom a Social Media Marketing Manager needs. It is just important to be sure that your team has common standards of Ethics!

social media plan

Now there is a real strategy plan behind it. The first thing you do is search engine optimization, search engine marketing and of course traditional marketing, we have to attract visitors to come to our website.

Web 2.0: Conversation
social media plan

And then we take care about usability, call to actions, special offers, dialogue marketing, so that the customer gets into contact with us and then he becomes a customer. And normal marketing ends here. And companies who belong to the 5%, who will survive all the difficult times, are those who say, this is not the end!

They go to the market, look at the customer and find out, where does the customer move, where does the customer live, where does he move in social media, for example in LinkedIn, in Facebook, YouTube, Twitter, and then they engage with them.

They start talking to him on events, on profile and fan pages, brand pages, talking, discussing, involving with this customer, with this one customer, because this customer knows other people who can also become customers, too. And the philosophy is always: the friends of my customers are potential customers.

Imagine all your customers just bringing one more customer to your business; imagine what will happen to your business! And this is exactly the power of social media. Then, social reputation management, that is what you really need, some central place in the headquarter maybe, that is only doing social media reputation management, looking who is writing what about our brand, about your product and then have a plan to react on it. The main thing is always, who in the company has the right to react and that has to be a person with a lot of empathy, don't take a choleric person, giving everyone only unnessary trouble.

Any questions? Ask us anything you like!

Fans get involved and fans do something very important, they not only visit your fan page, they visit your website, too!

And now imagine, this circle is moving and moving, you get new fans, get their addresses, get their contacts, find out where they are, find out their friends and then they all become visitors of your website! We were talking about the return on invest of your website: contacts per visitor.

We are getting more and more visitors out of our target group, out of our target defined customers, their contacts are sending their friends to our website, so that our return on invest of the website grows.

Imagine what happens if you do this ten times. That is exactly the power of the IROI way. If you follow this, you get automatically contacts out of your main target group, and that is really gold, and that is what has changed our traditional marketing completely.

> **iROI-Mindchange 61:** Facebook and Twitter are a good start, but we are moving at a high speed and it's not going to become less, because it's not a trend! It's a running train heading up very fast. Board it very soon!

Web 3.0: Confidence

Many companies have started developing this confidence system! This confidence system leads to a new art of innovation, it is called open innovation. Breaking up all the traditional borders in a company, where innovation was closed. What does that really mean?

Open Innovation

Example: A car company had this idea: "we are developing good cars, we are selling, but what we do is, we develop a car and then we try to find out a market, do marketing at the market and hope that some of our products will be bought. Hey, let's try it a different way, let's ask the customers, what they want, before building a new car!"

What they did was, they went online and asked all online users: "What type of car would you like to have?" People went into the Internet and built their car online, and the company built three of the winner cars in real, you know why?

After receiving 35.000 designs, 2.900 developers gave their ideas for free to the company and the company reserved more than 30 new patents while building these cars.

Can you imagine how cheap it was to get these patents?

What if you would create a huge funnel that would allow in all of the great new ideas? Like a giant idea vacuum, it would suck in everything and give you new ideas, you may never have dreamt of?

Any questions? Ask us anything you like!

Why should only a company have the ideas, the best ideas in their own company and not somewhere very far away?

Somebody giving the right idea for a product that sells like hot cakes? And that is what is happening, these are companies who have decided to resort to a mindchange:

> **iROI-Mindchange 62:** We don't know everything, we are ready to learn. If you are a customer and you want to improve our product, you are welcome.

It is a way of companies doing innovation in R&D (research & development) where they make much greater use of external ideas and technologies in their own business, and, in turn, let their unused ideas be used by others in *their* business. The old model of innovation was a closed model of innovation.

Think of a product development funnel turned on its side where ideas come from a science and technology base, are withered down and selected and taken to the market.

This is a classic technology push model. It worked very well for a long time in many industries, but these days, there is too much useful knowledge available in too many areas all over the world to try to do it all yourself.

Instead, what we need is an open model. So now we still have, in the Open Innovation Model, an R&D funnel turned on its side, but you will see there are many more pathways into the model for ideas to come in, not only from inside, but also from the outside.

Web 3.0: Confidence
innovation speed

And in turn, when those ideas are taken to the market, some of them go through to the company's own processes, but others go through other processes (think of licenses, spin-offs and joint ventures) to get to the market. So, in the Open Innovation model, it is much more open coming in, and much more open coming out.

Bosch started open innovation. You know what they did? "It is your refrigerator, can you improve it? Do you have any remarks? Give us the benefit of your ideas, we are stupid, you customer are the king, you were always the king, but we never dared to ask you and now you can do it online".

And the customers are giving their ideas online and they love it. And as soon as an idea is implemented, you know what grows?

innovation speed

But that has something to do with self-confidence! For open innovation to mean more than lip service, collaboration can't be one-sided. I remember one supplier road show. Fifteen vendors flew in from across the country and were each given ten minutes to pitch ideas based on a briefing we had sent.

We reviewed their presentations like reality show judges. We picked one winning idea, dismissed the others, and then browbeat the winning vendor on cost. This was a partnership in name only. Open innovation is not only about process. It's about mindset! I had to change the complete rules of this company – it would have died with this culture!

Any questions? Ask us anything you like!

> **iROI-Mindchange 63:** We need a different mentality! CEOs have understood: the customers are the best developers of a product, of a brand, because they know what they want and if there are many people who accept this idea, then we should react!

If you would know that one million people like the idea that the color of your product should be red, wouldn't you start producing it in red?

And that's it, this is changing our society, more and more. Bosch is asking people: "Hey, tell us how the next refrigerator should be? We shall build better refrigerators for you." They won't have to sell, people will be buying them automatically.

And that's the real difference, that is a real, again, a giant step in the evolution! We have to start asking and that is the potential, start building fans on your Facebook profiles, on your Twitter profiles, everywhere, LinkedIn, these people we will need one day when we are reaching web 3.0 to ask them what they want.

And this web 3.0, it's a real big advance, it's a real big change, because it changes our development cycle. If you want you can visit YouTube and just type in "*open innovation sauldie*" and then you can find a 60 minutes speech on open innovation at the Deutsche Telekom, the German telephone agency. Sorry, it is in German!

Web 3.0: Confidence
innovation speed

If you register this book on my website I will be providing an English version soon!

It's very important for you to understand, that this is not fun what we are talking about, this has direct impact on the future of the product development. If we ask the customer, we are the kings and the customer gives us the honor, he is also the king, but the first time we meet on an equal footing, as kings!

> **iROI-Mindchange 64:** We are kings. We are asking other kings to help us. And you know they are all ready to help you – the customer is the king – it was never so true like in digital times!

Give it a try! Join hands with us and we can help you rock your business!

Now we are moving to Web 4.0.

Web 4.0: Continuity: internet of things

In the Internet of Things, basically everything can be connected to the Internet. Every 'Thing' becomes a small computer that communicates with other Things. Communication between computers has evolved significantly over time. It started with electronic data interchange (EDI). Computers communicated over the Internet and then mobile phones got Internet access, and in the future things will have Internet access. Other authors mention more potential uses of the Internet of Things (International Telecommunication Union, 2005: 12; Casaleggio Associati, 2011: 3; Mattern, 2009: 4; 22; 14):

- Smart packaged food that communicates with the microwave the time needed to warm it up;

- Cars that give automatic warnings if a part of the car needs to be fixed;

- Wireless transmission of driver's license and passport information at borders, so that cars don't have to stop for the passport control at the border;

- Running shoes which communicate time, speed and distance so that runners can compete in real time with others on the other side of the world;

- Plants communicate to the sprinkler system when it's time for them to be watered.

Web 4.0: Continuity: internet of things
innovation speed

This last example actually already exists in some form. Called Botanicalls, it basically is a sensor that you can put in your plant at home, and the sensor monitors when the plant needs water. The sensor is connected to the Internet and sends the plant-owner Tweets on Twitter like "water me please", you didn't water me enough" or "thank you for watering me" (botanicalls.com).

What will be next? Stay tuned and connect yourself on my webpage **www.sauldie.org/vip** – there you can register this book and access daily updated news and information for your business!

Appendix

Search engine optimization checklist

Our research with over 50.000 Websites, that are on the Top of Google Rankings, reflected the following rules. You can tick those solved for your website!

- ☐ W3C compliant website coding/programming
- ☐ Programmed without Flash
- ☐ Programmed without frames
- ☐ there is more content than only that in inline frames
- ☐ Call to Action is defined clearly
- ☐ Automation of request response
- ☐ Automating email marketing with follow up emails
- ☐ Email marketing strategy with linking strategy
- ☐ Define automatic follow up emails
- ☐ Automatic measuring of reaction/response with A/B tests
- ☐ Layout according to iROI: 3 columns design, call to action on the right, navigation on the left, standard navigation on the top
- ☐ List of keywords updated regularly
- ☐ Input of titles from optimized keyword list
- ☐ Input of meta description from optimized keyword list
- ☐ Ticket system for customer requests
- ☐ Mobile version for iPad, iPhone and android
- ☐ Separated blog area with at least one new relevant entry per week related to the topic/subject.
- ☐ Having at least one keyword domain with a 301 redirect
- ☐ Set up of Google Alerts for the most important keywords
- ☐ Set up of an analytics tool (Google analytics or PIWIK)

Free downloads and more: www.sauldie.org/vip

Appendix
Search engine optimization checklist

- [ ] Intelligent search box: minor spelling errors will be ignored
- [ ] Intelligent search box: the URL can be read by Google
- [ ] Intelligent search box: search terms on the website are recorded in a database
- [ ] Glossary with terms/technical terms related to business
- [ ] QR - code for scanning on website for every page
- [ ] Integration of Google maps
- [ ] Linking of author with Google Plus
- [ ] Providing/controlling RSS feeds for/via categories
- [ ] Short URL as link and text link for Twitter and Google+
- [ ] Main URL optimized according to SEO
- [ ] Age of domain
- [ ] Number of web server neighbors
- [ ] Quality of web server neighbors
- [ ] Connection to internet of web server
- [ ] Pictures optimized by picture name
- [ ] Pictures optimized by alt attribute
- [ ] Pictures optimized by title attribute
- [ ] Pictures organized in gallery
- [ ] Individual linked keyword cloud on each page
- [ ] Tagging system with keywords
- [ ] Google Plus conformal evaluation
- [ ] Author function for Google search results
- [ ] Print function —print optimized pages as PDFs
- [ ] Optimized according to plugin SEO Doctor for Firefox
- [ ] Linking to related entries (internal links)
- [ ] Linking to external entries (external links)
- [ ] Linking from external websites/pages to website
- [ ] Linking from News—Sites (e.g. openpr) to website
- [ ] Linking from subject related forums to website

Any questions? Ask us anything you like!

Appendix
Search engine optimization checklist

- ☐ Linking from web catalogues to website
- ☐ Linking from blogs to website
- ☐ Linking from Wikipedia to special topics on website
- ☐ Embedding at least one YouTube video
- ☐ Embedding of at least one amazon link
- ☐ Text structure: max. 5% keyword density
- ☐ Text structure: exactly one h1—heading
- ☐ Text structure: several h2—headings
- ☐ Text structure: if required several h3—headings
- ☐ Text structure: quantity of words in text, "content is king"
- ☐ Optimizing: position of keyword in title
- ☐ Optimizing: position of keyword in description
- ☐ Link from YouTube video to website/landing page
- ☐ Linking to glossary from selected terms
- ☐ Linking to social bookmark websites
- ☐ Option to share on Facebook
- ☐ Option to mention on Twitter
- ☐ Option to connect via XING
- ☐ Option to share on Google Plus
- ☐ Automatic connection of articles to Facebook fan pages
- ☐ Automatic connection to Twitter accounts
- ☐ Automatic connection to LinkedIn
- ☐ Automatic publishing on XING
- ☐ Automatic publishing on Google Plus
- ☐ Automatic connection of YouTube channel
- ☐ In addition to automatic posts comment on or like other entries at least one time per day
- ☐ Start at most 10 new friend request per day
- ☐ Regular activity on all accounts
- ☐ Age of account

Appendix
Search engine optimization checklist

- ☐ Own blog on eblogger with RSS feed
- ☐ Checking social media reputation
- ☐ Checking of social media mentions
- ☐ Reactions on social media mentions
- ☐ Back office
- ☐ Creating/registering all accounts
- ☐ Central management of all accounts
- ☐ Merge data, so that all data and contacts from Facebook, Twitter, XING, LinkedIn andGoogle Plus are recorded in one data base
- ☐ Enter all business locations in Google Maps and link from Google Maps to respective company pages
- ☐ Measure server downtime and check website's reachability
- ☐ Always stay up to date!

Any questions? Ask us anything you like!

Appendix
Thank you so much!

Thank you so much!

Thanks for all the suggestions and great experiences which I get in coachings, speeches and seminars with CEOs.

Get to know me personally!

It would be a great pleasure for me!

Free downloads and more: www.sauldie.org/vip

Appendix
we support snehalaya

we support snehalaya

We are here to make sure basic human rights are ensured to people who are poor, destitute and uncared for. We believe everyone has the right to live a full life in freedom, good health and with access to education. We deliver pathfinding support and real opportunities to our clients to reintergrate in society.

Our organisation has been formed by strong and passionate individuals and many of us first found Snehalaya ourselves as clients and volunteers. Our organisation strives for social change and directly addresses society at large.

We primarily support Women & Children in Rural India, adversely affected by the commercial sex industry. Path-finding projects are formed on a need driven basis.

More information online:

http://www.snehalaya.de and http://www.snehankur.de
https://www.facebook.com/Snehalaya

Any questions? Ask us anything you like!

we support SOS-Kinderdörfer

Bye bye, dear reader – stay conected!

If you like this book and want to stay connected, click on **http://social.sauldie.org**

http://sauldie.org/author/sauldie/feed

https://plus.google.com/+SanjaySauldie/posts

http://twitter.com/topredner

https://www.facebook.com/sauldie

http://twitter.com/topredner

https://www.xing.com/profile/Sanjay_Sauldie

https://www.youtube.com/user/sauldie/videos

or send an email to english@sauldie.com or just give me a call: **+49 (0) 621 – 97 87 933**

Book Sanjay Sauldie as speaker or as coach

The astounding growth of the Internet has slashed the effectiveness of formerly dependable marketing channels. At the same time, the Internet has also enabled highly-targeted, cost-effective and remarkably accountable forms of marketing that simply didn't exist before. Any company that wants to attract and retain customers now needs to be mapping out and implementing the effective iROI-internet marketing strategy.

The iROI-keynote/speech/coaching lays the foundation for a practical understanding of the key components of internet marketing, including the best of the iROI-Strategy and in addition:

- The essential strategies upon which all successful internet marketing campaigns are based

- Valuable tips, tricks and resources that are based on real world experience – from analyzing over 500 companies

- Strategies in Internet Marketing, Social Media, Big Data and Smart Data, Customer Journey, Digital Leadership

Send an email to **english@sauldie.com** or just give me a call: **+49 (0) 621 – 97 87 933**